THE 160 DAY JOURNEY

From Fear to Faith

From Crisis to Calling: A 160-Day Journey from Fear and Doubt to Faith and Abundance.

JESSEE LOVAAS

ISBN: 979-8-9991423-0-6
Printed in the United States of America

Cover and interior design by Jessee Lovaas

ABOUT THE AUTHOR

Jessee Lovaas is a writer, speaker, and encourager with a heart for helping people rediscover purpose and peace. Whether through stories, Scripture, or quiet encouragement, he aims to point others back to hope and faith, and away from fear and doubt.

Jesse is the husband of a fantastic wife, Rebekah. He's a father of two beautiful kiddos, Henry and Savannah. And, he's a pet dad to Copper, the 14-year-old family Puggle.

www.Renew4d.com
Follow me @Renew4d
Instagram / Facebook / TikTok / Youtube / X / LinkedIn

To those walking through the wilderness and waiting for a breakthrough.

You are not alone. Walk with me from fear to faith.

Fear is a liar!

INTRODUCTION

This devotional was born out of seasons of struggle, stillness, and learning to hear God's voice in the quiet. Each day is a step toward healing, toward hope, toward renewal. You don't have to be perfect to start. You just have to begin.

A myriad of feelings and emotions have arisen throughout the COVID-19 pandemic. But through God's love and Jesus' sacrifice, I can stand today with complete confidence and declare (along with 1 Corinthians 10:13 TPT) that we will not be given more than we can handle, and that God WILL make a way of escape. I do not fear what is happening, because my hope is in something much greater than a virus or lack of toilet paper.

This 160-day journey began with the Holy Spirit convicting me about my social media output regarding the pandemic and COVID-19. The Lord prompted me to start sharing the Gospel and words of encouragement on a daily basis. I did not know how long it would last, but God did. And for 160 days, the Holy Spirit brought new revelation and blessing upon my life in a new and radical way, ways that I would have never thought possible. So if you think you're on a long, dark road, join me in this 160-day devotional. It will encourage, teach, build up, tear down, convict, bless, and ultimately, my hope, build a new level of faith and hope in your life that you've never experienced before.

My challenge to anyone who reads this is to participate. And find a way to share your own words of encouragement or testimonies yourself. Let God's love and mighty works be displayed across social media and in your life, rather than the political doomsaying negativity that currently headlines. If you do not know God, or are unchurched, or have been hurt in the past, I challenge you to at least read some "good news" each day and think how your life, or a hurting friend or family members life, could be different with a bit of faith or a miracle in your life. Know you are loved, thought of, created for purpose, and have so much to offer this world. Try to smile. Look up to Heaven and just marvel at the good things in your life.

I'll leave you with this. COVID was a crazy season of disease, job loss, stock market crash, and worry. Fast forward a few years to 2025, and politically and economically, not much has changed. FEAR NOT! Isaiah 43:1 tells us not to fear. Fear is a Liar!

I felt the Lord break this 160-day journey into four seasons. Each season lasted around 40 days.

The 1st 40 days were a season of protection.

This was a season of protection. I found the Lord protecting my mind, thoughts, and heart. God's grace quickly overtook any worry, doubt, or fear during this season. He fought for me so I could work on renewing my mind and getting my heart and spirit right.

The 2nd 40 days were a season of temptation.

After a season of strengthening and renewal, I was immediately struck by temptation. Not so much sin, but more so temptation to go back to the "old life" or old way of thinking. I was tempted by fear and lack. But God's word prevailed during this season!

The 3rd 40 days were a season of preparation and training.

This season came a hard-nosed, blue-collar, gets-your-hands-dirty season of preparation. I knew God was doing a massive work in me, and this 40-day season was preparing my mind and hands for what God was leading me into. This is the "you're either in or out" phase. It's a challenging phase because victory is on the other side if you persevere.

The 4th 40 days were a season of new life and victory!

This season was a season of refreshing, renewal, and victory. I saw finances break forth. I saw debt released. I saw victory in my life over areas of sin, doubt, and fear. What came out of the final season of this journey was a "new birth". I was renewed and made new. I had momentum heading into the new season after the COVID-19 pandemic.

Now, why did the Lord lead me through 4 seasons of 40? In the Bible, the number 40 and periods of 40 days or 40 years are often used symbolically to represent a time of trial, probation, testing, and renewal. It's not necessarily a literal or exact duration, but rather a period of significant change or preparation. The number 40 in the bible is substantial. 40 days can also symbolize a period of transformation, growth, and the emergence of new life or a new beginning. Each season of 40 throughout this devotional does just that. Each season is different, yet still just as transformative as the last.

Examples in the Bible:
- Noah's Flood: The rain lasted 40 days and 40 nights, representing a cleansing and a new beginning for the world.
- Moses on Mount Sinai: Moses fasted and spent 40 days on Mount Sinai, receiving the Law, which marked a period of intense communion with God and the establishment of the covenant.
- Jesus in the Wilderness: Jesus fasted and was tempted by the devil for 40 days in the wilderness, preparing him for his ministry.
- Israelites in the Wilderness: They wandered in the desert for 40 years, undergoing a period of testing and preparation before entering the Promised Land.
- The 40 days of Lent in Christianity are rooted in the biblical usage of 40, symbolizing a period of fasting, prayer, and penance as a time of spiritual preparation for the celebration of Jesus's resurrection.

Public Service Announcement

If at some point you feel like you've seen a passage of scripture before, you're probably right. Trust me, it deceived me as well. But what I noticed is that throughout the 160 days, you experience different seasons and different impacts a verse has. So, you might see a particular verse two or three times. But I assure you that each time you visit a verse, it will have a different impact and different meaning for that particular season.

From crisis to calling. This 160-day journey from fear and doubt to faith and abundance starts now!

Each entry includes a Scripture, a reflection, a short prayer, and a journaling prompt. Set aside time each day to read, reflect, and respond. Let God meet you in these pages.

This isn't a checklist. It's a conversation. One day at a time.

SEASON 1

~ The 1st 40 days ~

A season of protection.

Day 1: Fear Is a Liar

Scripture
Isaiah 43:1

Reflection
This past Sunday, my pastor shared how disappointing it was to see that very few people posted Scripture, encouragement, or prayers on social media during the pandemic's chaos. Instead, negativity and fear dominated our timelines. I felt convicted. Though I tried to stay lighthearted, I realized I was contributing to the noise rather than standing out in faith. Social media is powerful, and in my previous role, I utilized it to lead, connect, and uplift people. So why not do the same now? I made a decision: from now on, I will share God's Word, encouragement, and hope. Not politics or fear-mongering. The Great Commission isn't about converting everyone—it's about making sure everyone hears the truth. I am a man of God—not perfect, but striving daily. And I believe, as 1 Corinthians 10:13 says, God will make a way through every trial. Our hope is greater than any virus or shortage. In this storm, we are called to shine. To love. You are created for a purpose. You are not alone. Lift your eyes, take a deep breath, and remember: fear is a liar, and God is in control.

Prayer
Lord, help me not to fear. Let me rest in the knowledge that I am Yours and You are with me always. Give me peace that surpasses all understanding.

Journal Prompt
What fears are you currently facing, and how can you surrender them to God today?

My Notes & Prayers

_____

_____

_____

_____

_____

Day 2: Surrounded by Angels

Scripture
2 Kings 6:16

Reflection
Ephesians 6:12 reminds us that we are not wrestling against flesh and blood, but against spiritual forces of darkness. Right now, with the chaos of the coronavirus, it can feel like we're surrounded by a real and tangible enemy—fear, disease, financial loss, division. But just like Elisha's servant in 2 Kings 6, we need our spiritual eyes opened to see the armies of Heaven surrounding and protecting us. God is still on the throne. We are not alone. As believers, our response must be spiritual first: pray, worship, trust, and intercede. We must remember that God sends His angels to protect and deliver. Let's stop fighting people on social media and instead focus on fighting the spiritual battle with prayer and truth. Let our words lift up instead of tear down. Let our focus be unity, compassion, and trust in God's greater plan. Even when we feel surrounded, we are surrounded by God.

Prayer
Father, open my eyes to see that You are fighting for me. Help me not to fear, but to trust in Your unseen protection and care.

Journal Prompt
What's one area where you feel outnumbered or overwhelmed? Write a prayer asking for God's help.

My Notes & Prayers

_____

_____

_____

_____

_____

Day 3: Don't Shrink Back

Scripture
Hebrews 10:39

Reflection
In times of crisis, the natural instinct is to protect ourselves—hoard resources, retreat, or stop giving. But Hebrews 10:39 urges us not to shrink back. We are not like those who draw back in fear, but those who press forward in faith. Faith is not just believing when things are easy, but acting with trust when everything around us looks uncertain. The parable of the talents in Matthew 25 teaches us that when we invest and steward what God has given us, even when it's risky, He rewards us. Fear tells us to bury what we have. Faith calls us to sow generously, trust God, and be wise stewards. In my own life, I've experienced profound loss and financial strain, but I've learned that God honors faithful living. He provides. We can stand firm on His promises and walk forward, knowing He multiplies what we offer Him.

Prayer
Jesus, help me to keep stepping forward even when it's hard. Give me the faith to trust You with my future.

Journal Prompt
Are you shrinking back or stepping forward in this season? Why?

My Notes & Prayers

_____

_____

_____

_____

_____

Day 4: It is Well When I Wait

Scripture
Isaiah 40:31

Reflection
Waiting on God is often one of the hardest spiritual disciplines. Isaiah 40:31 encourages us that those who wait on the Lord will renew their strength. Waiting is not inactivity—it's a time of spiritual preparation. During quarantine, our lives slowed down in unexpected ways. We have more time at home, more quiet moments, and more opportunities to seek God's presence. Biblical waiting is active. It involves prayer, meditation, worship, and listening. Just as Moses met with God in the cave and was transformed, we, too, can encounter God in our 'caves' of isolation. Don't waste this season on Netflix and distractions. Use it to go deeper. Seek God's heart. Hear His voice. Receive His peace. In the quiet, He speaks loudest.

Prayer
Lord, teach me how to wait on You. In stillness and prayer, let me be renewed and restored.

Journal Prompt
How can you wait *actively* this week? What might that look like?

My Notes & Prayers

_____

_____

_____

_____

_____

Day 5: Youth Gone Wild

📖 Scripture
Jeremiah 29:11

💬 Reflection
The youth of this generation are facing a moment in history that will shape them forever. Seniors have missed milestone events: prom, graduation, and last games. For them, it's heartbreaking. As adults, we must not dismiss their pain or minimize their experience. Jeremiah 29:11 reminds us that God still has a future and hope for them. Our role is to empathize, encourage, and pour into their lives. They're watching how we react, how we lead, how we love. Let us be present examples of Christ during this season. Let them see joy, faith, and purpose in us—even in hard times. Invest in them spiritually. Speak life over them. Make memories with them. Point them toward God's promises and purpose for their lives.

🙏 Prayer
God, give me compassion and wisdom to support the youth in my life. Help me reflect Your love through my words and actions.

✏️ Journal Prompt
Think of a teen or student you know. Write a short note or prayer of encouragement for them.

✍️ My Notes & Prayers

_____

_____

_____

_____

_____

Day 6: Light in the Kingdom

Scripture
Matthew 5:14

Reflection
We are called to be a light to the world, not just in word, but in how we live. Matthew 5 says we are a city on a hill, a lamp on a stand. The world is watching, especially in times of darkness. Our reactions, our kindness, our generosity—these things reflect Jesus. In the Old Testament, the high priest wore a breastplate with twelve precious stones—each representing a tribe of Israel. When God's presence filled the Holy of Holies, imagine the light shining through those stones, creating a dazzling display. That's how our lives should look—radiating God's light in colorful, unmistakable ways. We're not meant to blend in, but to stand out. In a black-and-white world, God's people should live in vibrant color. Let His light shine through every word and deed.

Prayer
Jesus, let Your light shine through me. Remove anything that dims my witness, and help me live in holy color and contrast to this dark world.

Journal Prompt
What's one way you can be a light in your home, workplace, or online?

My Notes & Prayers

_____

_____

_____

_____

_____

Day 7: Let's Be the Church

📖 Scripture
James 5:13

💬 Reflection
Church is not confined to a building—it's the people of God living out faith wherever they are. James 5:13 tells us to pray in suffering and sing in joy. In this season, many churches are streaming online, meeting in homes, and worshipping in new ways. This is an opportunity to redefine what it means to be the church. It's not about a stage, a microphone, or a perfect set list—it's about people coming together in unity, prayer, and praise. Let your living room become a sanctuary. Let your voice echo with worship. Let your neighbors hear your hope. In times of uncertainty, the church shines brightest when it leaves the building and becomes the hands and feet of Christ.

🙏 Prayer
Father, thank You for making me part of Your church. Let my home be filled with praise and my life be a reflection of You.

✏️ Journal Prompt
How can you *be the church* to someone today?

🕊️ My Notes & Prayers

_____

_____

_____

_____

_____

Day 8: Tests & Mess

Scripture

Philippians 1:12

Reflection

Life can throw us into unexpected valleys—trials that feel unfair or even unbearable. But God never wastes pain. What was meant to harm you, He can use to shape your purpose. Paul was imprisoned, yet he declared that his situation actually served to advance the gospel. That's the beauty of God's economy—He turns tests into testimonies and messes into messages. If the enemy is targeting you, it's likely because your calling threatens him. Instead of asking 'Why me?', ask 'What's next, Lord?' Trust that what you go through today may be what sets someone else free tomorrow. Your breakthrough isn't just for you—it's for others watching your life.

Prayer

Lord, help me to see purpose in my pain. Use my trials to shape a testimony that brings others to you.

Journal Prompt

What part of your story might God use to help someone else?

My Notes & Prayers

_____

_____

_____

_____

_____

Day 9: It's OK To Rest

Scripture

Isaiah 40:31

Reflection

We live in a world that idolizes hustle. Rest often feels like weakness. But Scripture teaches the opposite. Isaiah reminds us that those who wait on the Lord will renew their strength, not those who never stop, but those who pause in God's presence. Even Jesus rested. He took time away to pray, sleep, and be alone with the Father. Rest is holy. Rest is obedience. If you are tired this season, allow yourself the grace to slow down. Take time to breathe, pray, and let God refill you. Rest doesn't mean giving up; it means trusting that God is still working, even when you're not.

Prayer

Father, I give You my exhaustion. Help me to rest in Your promises and let go of constant striving.

Journal Prompt

What is one way you can intentionally rest this week?

My Notes & Prayers

_____

_____

_____

_____

_____

Day 10: His Promises Are Yes and Amen

Scripture

2 Corinthians 1:20

Reflection

God never breaks a promise. His Word is full of truths we can stand on—even when our circumstances scream otherwise. In times of loss or confusion, remember: He is the Author and Finisher of your faith. His promises aren't vague hopes—His character guarantees them. Maybe you've been waiting for something for a long time. Perhaps you feel forgotten. You're not. God hasn't missed one detail of your life. If He said it, He will do it. Don't lose faith in the waiting. Let His promises become your anchor. Declare them. Believe them. Live like they're already coming to pass.

Prayer

Lord, I trust Your Word. Strengthen my faith to believe every promise You've made, even when I can't yet see it.

Journal Prompt

Which promise of God do you need to hold onto right now?

My Notes & Prayers

_____

_____

_____

_____

_____

Day 11: Where You Go I'll Go

Scripture

Exodus 33:15

Reflection

Moses understood something powerful—God's presence is more valuable than any destination. He said, 'If Your presence does not go with us, do not bring us up from here.' It's easy to chase goals, jobs, or relationships and forget to ask if God is in them. But His presence is what gives those things purpose. If He's not leading the way, we're just wandering. Invite God into every decision. Refuse to go where He isn't. That's where peace lives—in the center of His will.

Prayer

Jesus, guide my steps. Don't let me move ahead of you or apart from you. I only want what you are in.

Journal Prompt

Are there areas in your life where you're moving ahead of God?

My Notes & Prayers

_____

_____

_____

_____

_____

Day 12: All I Can Do Is Pray

📖 Scripture

James 5:16

💬 Reflection

When tragedy strikes, we often feel helpless. We say things like, 'All I can do is pray,' as if prayer is a last resort. But in truth, prayer is the greatest thing we can do. Prayer moves Heaven. It aligns our hearts with God's. It opens doors, breaks chains, and brings peace. Never underestimate its power. You don't have to have the right words—just a willing heart. God hears. God cares. And God responds. Let prayer be your first response, not your final option.

🙏 Prayer

Lord, teach me to pray without ceasing. Let me believe in the power of my prayers, because they reach your heart.

✏️ Journal Prompt

Who or what do you need to pray for more consistently?

🖊️ My Notes & Prayers

_____

_____

_____

_____

_____

Day 13: Your Weakness Promotes God's Strength

Scripture

2 Corinthians 12:9

Reflection

We don't like to talk about our weaknesses. We hide them. But Paul boasted in his. Why? Because he knew that God's power shows up strongest when we admit our lack. You don't have to have it all together. You just have to surrender. When you're tired, discouraged, or worn down, God shows up with supernatural strength. Don't be ashamed of your limits. God is glorified in them. Today, bring Him your exhaustion and let Him fill you with His grace.

Prayer

Jesus, I give You my weakness. Let Your strength rise in me and carry me through today.

Journal Prompt

What weakness can you surrender to God right now?

My Notes & Prayers

_____

_____

_____

_____

_____

Day 14: My Hope Is In You

Scripture

Hebrews 11:1

Reflection

Hope is not wishful thinking—it's confident expectation in a faithful God. When everything else feels unstable, hope remains. Not because of what we see, but because of who we trust. The world is full of uncertainty, but God's promises never change. Let hope rise in your heart today. Let it be stronger than fear, louder than doubt, and more persistent than disappointment. Hope is your anchor. Hold onto it. Let it remind you that God's best is yet to come.

Prayer

God, restore my hope. Let it anchor me in this season and pull me forward into Your promises.

Journal Prompt

Write a hope-filled declaration over your life today.

My Notes & Prayers

_____

_____

_____

_____

_____

Day 15: Stillness Speaks

Scripture

Psalm 46:10

Reflection

Be still and know that I am God. This verse isn't a gentle suggestion; it's a command. In the middle of chaos, God calls us to stillness. When we quiet the noise, we create space to hear His voice. Stillness isn't inactivity—it's trust. It's laying down our need to control and choosing to rest in God's sovereignty. When the world gets loud, God whispers. Don't miss His voice because you're drowning in distractions. Pause. Breathe. Listen. He's already at work in your waiting.

Prayer

God, teach me to be still in Your presence. Quiet the noise in my heart so I can hear Your voice.

Journal Prompt

Where do you need to practice stillness in your life this week?

My Notes & Prayers

_____

_____

_____

_____

_____

Day 16: Peace Like a River

Scripture

Isaiah 66:12

Reflection

God promises to extend peace to us like a river. Rivers aren't stagnant—they move, flow, and shape the land they pass through. His peace is active. It doesn't mean the absence of trouble, but the presence of assurance in the middle of it. Let His peace carry you forward. Trust that even in the bends and rapids of life, His current is steady, strong, and sure.

Prayer

Lord, let Your peace wash over me. Guide me like a river, steady and full of grace.

Journal Prompt

What would it look like for God's peace to 'flow' through your day today?

My Notes & Prayers

_____

_____

_____

_____

_____

Day 17: The Anchor Holds

Scripture

Hebrews 6:19

Reflection

Hope is the anchor for our souls. It keeps us grounded when storms rage. An anchor doesn't stop the storm—it holds you steady through it. Jesus is our hope. When everything feels uncertain, He is our constant. Don't focus on the waves. Fix your eyes on the Anchor. He won't let go.

Prayer

Jesus, You are my Anchor. Keep me steady in faith, even when life feels shaky.

Journal Prompt

What storm are you facing, and how can you cling to your Anchor today?

My Notes & Prayers

_____

_____

_____

_____

_____

Day 18: Calm in the Chaos

Scripture

Mark 4:39

Reflection

Jesus calmed the storm with three words: 'Peace, be still.' He spoke to the wind and waves, and they obeyed. That same voice speaks to your storm. No matter how violent the winds or how high the waves, Jesus is in your boat. He is not panicked. He is present. Call on Him. Invite Him to speak peace over your chaos. His authority calms every fear.

Prayer

Lord, speak peace over the storms in my life. Remind me that You are with me and in control.

Journal Prompt

Write a prayer asking Jesus to calm a specific area of chaos in your life.

My Notes & Prayers

_____

_____

_____

_____

_____

Day 19: He Sees You

Scripture

Genesis 16:13

Reflection

Hagar felt invisible and abandoned, yet God saw her. She called Him 'the God who sees me.' In your darkest, loneliest moments, God sees you, too. You are never out of His sight, never out of His reach. He knows your name, your pain, your fear. And He cares. His eyes are on you. Rest in the truth that you are seen, known, and loved.

Prayer

Father, thank You for seeing me when I feel unseen. Remind me daily that I am not forgotten.

Journal Prompt

Where have you been feeling overlooked? Invite God into that place today.

My Notes & Prayers

_____

_____

_____

_____

_____

Day 20: From Panic to Prayer

Scripture

Philippians 4:6-7

Reflection

Anxiety doesn't have to own you. Paul tells us to bring everything—every fear, every need—to God in prayer. When we do, peace guards our hearts and minds. Panic says, 'What if?' Prayer says, 'Even if.' Let your worry become worship. Turn your panic into a prayer. God is listening, and He's ready to respond with peace.

Prayer

God, help me to bring my anxiety to You in prayer. Exchange my panic for Your peace.

Journal Prompt

What's one anxious thought you can turn into a prayer today?

My Notes & Prayers

_____

_____

_____

_____

_____

Day 21: The Battle Belongs to God

Scripture

2 Chronicles 20:15

Reflection

You don't have to fight every battle alone. The Lord told His people not to be afraid or discouraged, because the battle was His. When you feel overwhelmed, remind yourself: God fights for me. Stand firm. Worship. Trust. Watch what He will do on your behalf. Your job is not to win the battle, but to stay close to the One who already has.

Prayer

Lord, I surrender this battle to You. Fight for me, and give me peace as I wait on You.

Journal Prompt

What battle do you need to release into God's hands today?

My Notes & Prayers

_____

_____

_____

_____

_____

Day 22: What I See

Scripture

1 Samuel 16:7

Reflection

The world is quick to judge by appearance, status, or success. But God sees deeper. He looks at the heart—the unseen battles, the quiet strength, the unnoticed faith. You may not look the part to others, but God delights in who you are becoming. Don't let shallow judgments shape your identity. When you live for God's approval, external praise or criticism loses its power. God sees the intentions, the courage, and the growth that others overlook. He is not swayed by what impresses the world. Rest in the truth that God's gaze is fixed on your heart, and He calls it worthy.

Prayer

God, help me to care more about what You see in me than what others say about me. Change my focus from appearance to heart, from comparison to calling.

Journal Prompt

What part of your heart is God shaping that the world can't see?

My Notes & Prayers

_____

_____

_____

_____

_____

Day 23: Broken and Beautiful

📖 Scripture

2 Corinthians 4:7

💬 Reflection

We often try to hide our cracks, believing they disqualify us. But Scripture reminds us that we are jars of clay—fragile, yes, but filled with God's power. The cracks are where His light shines through. Your broken places don't make you useless; they make you human. And in God's hands, even brokenness becomes a platform for His glory. He doesn't ask for perfection—He asks for surrender. Bring Him the shattered parts, and watch Him create something beautiful.

🙏 Prayer

Lord, I bring You the parts of me that feel broken. Use them to reveal Your strength and grace. Let Your light shine through every crack.

✒️ Journal Prompt

How has God used a broken part of your story to bless others?

✍️ My Notes & Prayers

_____

_____

_____

_____

Day 24: Don't Look Back

Scripture

Philippians 3:13

Reflection

The past has a voice that tries to keep us stuck—regret, shame, nostalgia. But God calls us forward. Paul reminds us to forget what lies behind and press on. Healing doesn't come from reliving the past but from walking into God's future. You are not who you were. Don't let yesterday define you. Fix your eyes on what God is doing now and where He's leading you next. There is freedom in letting go and grace in moving forward.

Prayer

Jesus, help me release what's behind me. I fix my eyes on You and trust that what's ahead is filled with purpose and hope.

Journal Prompt

What do you need to stop looking back at to move forward?

My Notes & Prayers

_____

_____

_____

_____

_____

Day 25: Don't Be Afraid

Scripture

Joshua 1:9

Reflection

Courage isn't the absence of fear—it's moving forward despite it. God told Joshua to be strong and courageous, not because the path would be easy, but because He would be with him. You don't have to wait until you feel fearless to act in faith. Take the step while trembling. Say yes while uncertain. God's presence is your strength, not your own confidence. Fear will try to hold you back, but obedience will take you places fear never could.

Prayer

Lord, give me courage to do the hard things even when I'm afraid. Remind me You are with me, and that's all I need to move forward.

Journal Prompt

What step is God asking you to take today, even if you're scared?

My Notes & Prayers

_____

_____

_____

_____

_____

Day 26: Rooted

📖 Scripture

Jeremiah 17:7–8

💬 Reflection

A tree doesn't grow fruit without deep roots, and neither do we. Jeremiah reminds us that the one who trusts in the Lord is like a tree planted by water. In dry seasons, that tree still bears fruit because its roots run deep. Storms will come, heat will rise, but those who are rooted in God endure. What are you rooted in? If it's approval, control, or comfort, it will fail. But if it's God, you will thrive in any season. Dig deeper today. Let His Word water your soul.

🙏 Prayer

God, help me stay rooted in You. Grow my faith deep so I can flourish even when life is hard.

✏️ Journal Prompt

What spiritual habits are helping you grow deeper roots in this season?

✍️ My Notes & Prayers

_____

_____

_____

_____

_____

Day 27: Purpose in the Pain

Scripture

Romans 8:28

Reflection

Pain often feels pointless, but God wastes nothing. Romans 8:28 promises that all things—yes, even your pain—work together for good. This doesn't mean everything is good, but that God can bring purpose out of anything. Even when we don't see it, He is weaving redemption through our story. Your hurt is not hidden from Him. He's close to the brokenhearted, and He's building something beautiful out of your brokenness. Lean in. Trust His process. Healing and purpose are already in motion.

Prayer

Father, use my pain for Your glory. Help me to trust that You are working all things together for good, even when I can't see how.

Journal Prompt

How has God used a painful season in your life for good?

My Notes & Prayers

_____

_____

_____

_____

_____

Day 28: The Shepherd Knows

Scripture

John 10:14

Reflection

There's comfort in being fully known—and fully loved. Jesus says, "I am the good shepherd. I know My sheep." He knows your voice, your fears, and your struggles. He sees the things others overlook. He leads with compassion, not criticism. When you wander, He comes looking. You are not just one among many—you are deeply known and fiercely loved.

Prayer

Jesus, thank You for being my Shepherd. Help me to follow Your voice today and trust that You know what's best for me.

Journal Prompt

Where do you need to trust the Shepherd's voice in your life right now?

My Notes & Prayers

Day 29: Peace Is a Person

📖 Scripture

John 14:27

💬 Reflection

We often chase peace like it's a feeling to find. But real peace isn't found in circumstances—it's found in Christ. Jesus said, "My peace I give you." That means peace is not something we earn or manufacture. It's His gift, anchored in His presence. When life feels shaky, hold onto the One who never changes. Invite Him into your worry, and let His peace guard your heart.

🙏 Prayer

Lord, help me stop searching for peace in the wrong places. Fill me with Your peace today—the peace that only You can give.

✒️ Journal Prompt

What would it look like to receive peace as a gift instead of striving for it?

✍️ My Notes & Prayers

_____

_____

_____

_____

_____

Day 30: You Matter

Scripture

Psalm 139:13-14

Reflection

In a world full of comparison and noise, it's easy to feel invisible. But God says you are fearfully and wonderfully made. Every detail of you was crafted with care and intention. You are not an accident. You matter. To God, to the people around you, and the story being written right now. Don't underestimate the value of your presence. You were created on purpose for a purpose.

Prayer

God, thank You for creating me with a purpose. Remind me today that I matter—not because of what I do, but because of who I am in You.

Journal Prompt

What would change if you truly believed you were wonderfully made?

My Notes & Prayers

_____

_____

_____

_____

_____

Day 31: No Condemnation

Scripture

Romans 8:1

Reflection

Guilt says, "You're unworthy." Grace says, "You're forgiven." Romans 8:1 declares there is now no condemnation for those in Christ Jesus. That's a powerful promise. You don't have to live under shame anymore. Jesus took the weight of it on the cross. So stop punishing yourself for what He already paid for. You are free. Walk in that freedom today, not just in theory, but in heart and habit.

Prayer

Jesus, thank You for taking my shame and declaring me free. Help me to live in the truth that there is no condemnation in You.

Journal Prompt

Is there any guilt or shame you're holding onto that Jesus already forgave?

My Notes & Prayers

_____

_____

_____

_____

_____

Day 32: You Have a Helper

Scripture

John 14:26

Reflection

You're not doing this alone. Jesus sent the Holy Spirit as our Helper, our Advocate, and our Comforter. When life feels overwhelming or confusing, you have divine help. He reminds you of the truth, gives you wisdom, and strengthens you to do what you can't on your own. He is with you in the decision-making, the parenting, the healing, and the growth. You don't have to figure everything out alone. Pause and invite Him in. He will lead you with peace and empower you with grace. Your Helper is already here.

Prayer

Holy Spirit, I welcome You today. Help me remember I'm not alone. Guide my steps and speak truth into every part of my life.

Journal Prompt

Where do you need the Holy Spirit's help today?

My Notes & Prayers

_____

_____

_____

_____

_____

Day 33: One Step at a Time

Scripture

Psalm 119:105

Reflection

We often want the whole roadmap, but God gives us light for one step at a time. Psalm 119:105 reminds us that His Word is a lamp to our feet. That means He leads us moment by moment, not all at once. This keeps us close to Him. It teaches dependence, not control. If you don't know the whole plan, that's okay. You only need enough light to take the next right step. And with each step, He'll meet you there.

Prayer

Lord, help me to trust You with the next step. I don't need the whole picture—just Your light and Your presence.

Journal Prompt

What next step do you feel God is calling you to take today?

My Notes & Prayers

_____

_____

_____

_____

_____

Day 34: His Mercies Are New

Scripture

Lamentations 3:22-23

Reflection

Every morning, you wake up to a clean slate. God's mercies are new, not recycled, not leftover—brand new. You don't have to carry yesterday's mistakes into today. Grace meets you where you are and leads you forward. Shame may try to follow you, but mercy has already made a way. Receive it. Start again. This is a new day, and He is faithful in it.

Prayer

Father, thank You for new mercies today. I let go of yesterday and receive Your grace for what's ahead.

Journal Prompt

What mercy do you need to receive for today?

My Notes & Prayers

_____

_____

_____

_____

_____

Day 35: God Sees You Fully

Scripture

Psalm 33:13–15

Reflection

God doesn't just glance at you—He watches with deep understanding. Every breath, every burden, every battle is fully seen. When you feel like no one notices your pain, remember that God sees all of you—your effort, your tears, your hidden faithfulness. He is not a distant observer but an involved Father. His gaze is filled with compassion, not judgment. He sees where you are and also where you're going. Let the reality of His attentive love bring rest to your striving heart.

Prayer

Lord, thank You for truly seeing me. Help me remember I am never invisible to You.

Journal Prompt

When have you felt unnoticed, and how can you rest in God's attention today?

My Notes & Prayers

_____

_____

_____

_____

_____

Day 36: Freedom to Forgive

Scripture

Ephesians 4:32

Reflection

Forgiveness is not letting someone off the hook—it's setting yourself free. Bitterness chains us to the pain. But forgiveness breaks those chains. God calls us to forgive as we've been forgiven. Not because they deserve it, but because we are called to live free. You can forgive and still set boundaries. You can release the burden and leave justice to God. Today is a good day to stop carrying what He already carried for you.

Prayer

Lord, help me to forgive. Give me the strength to let go of bitterness and choose freedom through Your grace.

Journal Prompt

Who do you need to forgive—not for them, but for your freedom?

My Notes & Prayers

_____

_____

_____

_____

_____

Day 37: You're Not Too Far

Scripture

Luke 15:20

Reflection

No matter how far you've wandered, you are never out of God's reach. The story of the prodigal son reminds us that God runs toward us with open arms. He doesn't wait with crossed arms or condemnation—He moves in love. You may feel unworthy or ashamed, but God calls you His. He restores what was broken and rejoices when you return. You don't have to clean yourself up first. Just come home.

Prayer

Father, thank You for pursuing me even when I wander. Draw me back to Your love and remind me that I'm never too far from grace.

Journal Prompt

What do you need to return to God with today?

My Notes & Prayers

_____

_____

_____

_____

_____

Day 38: God Is With You

Scripture

Isaiah 41:10

Reflection

Fear often lies in telling us we are alone. But God's Word declares, 'Do not fear, for I am with you.' That promise is more than comfort—it's strength. He's not just near, He's actively helping and upholding you. In the uncertainty, in the waiting, in the pain—He is with you. You may not feel it, but His presence never leaves. Lean on Him today. He will hold you up when you can't stand on your own.

Prayer

God, thank You for being with me. Remind me in every moment that I am not alone. Help me to feel Your presence today.

Journal Prompt

Where in your life do you need to trust that God is with you?

My Notes & Prayers

_____

_____

_____

_____

_____

Day 39: Strength in Surrender

Scripture

2 Corinthians 12:9

Reflection

We try to be strong, to keep it all together, but true strength is found in surrender. God's grace is made perfect in our weakness. That means you don't have to pretend you're okay. You can bring your weakness to God and find power there. You're not failing by needing Him—you're living by faith. Lay it all down. Let His grace carry what you can't.

Prayer

Jesus, I surrender my weakness to You. Be strong where I am not, and help me rest in Your grace.

Journal Prompt

What area of your life do you need to stop trying to carry alone?

My Notes & Prayers

_____

_____

_____

_____

_____

Day 40: Speak His Promises

Scripture

Isaiah 55:11

Reflection

God's Word doesn't return empty—it accomplishes what He sends it to
do. When you speak His promises over your life, you're not just
reciting words—you're releasing truth. Scripture has the power to shift
your mindset, silence lies, and stir hope. Don't just think it—speak it.
Declare His truth even when your feelings disagree. Let His Word
shape your reality, not your circumstances.

Prayer

Lord, help me speak Your promises over my life. Fill my heart with
truth and let it overflow in my words today.

Journal Prompt

What is one Bible verse you can speak over your life today?

My Notes & Prayers

_____

_____

_____

_____

_____

SEASON 2

~ The 2nd 40 days ~

A season of temptation.

Day 41: Worthy of Love

Scripture

Romans 5:8

Reflection

God didn't wait for you to get it all together before He loved you.
Romans 5:8 says He demonstrated His love while we were still
sinners. You are not loved because you're perfect—you're loved
because He is love. You don't have to earn it. You just have to receive
it. Let His love redefine your worth today.

Prayer

Jesus, thank You for loving me in my worst moments. Teach me to
receive Your love and believe I'm worthy of it because You said so.

Journal Prompt

What keeps you from believing God fully loves you?

My Notes & Prayers

_____

_____

_____

_____

_____

Day 42: God Is Still Writing

Scripture

Philippians 1:6

Reflection

God doesn't start stories He doesn't plan to finish. Whatever He began in you, He will carry it through. Even when progress feels slow or messy, He is still working. Your story isn't stuck—it's still being written. Trust the Author. He knows the ending, and it's full of purpose and hope.

Prayer

Father, thank You for writing my story. Help me trust You in the unfinished parts and believe that You're not done with me yet.

Journal Prompt

What part of your story are you still learning to trust God with?

My Notes & Prayers

_____

_____

_____

_____

_____

Day 43: Hold On

Scripture

Galatians 6:9

Reflection

Weariness can make you want to give up right before the breakthrough. But Galatians 6:9 reminds us that in due time, we will reap a harvest—if we do not give up. God sees your persistence. He knows the prayers you've prayed, the tears you've cried, the seeds you've sown. Your labor is not in vain. Sometimes growth is invisible before it's undeniable. So don't let fatigue talk you out of faith. Keep going. The harvest is coming.

Prayer

God, when I feel weary, help me to hold on. Give me the strength to keep planting seeds of faith and trusting in Your timing.

Journal Prompt

Where in your life do you need to keep going instead of giving up?

My Notes & Prayers

_____

_____

_____

_____

_____

Day 44: Still Good

Scripture

Psalm 34:8

Reflection

Life may not always feel good, but God still is. Psalm 34:8 invites us to taste and see that the Lord is good. Sometimes we need to pause and intentionally remember His goodness. Look back at His faithfulness. Pay attention to small gifts in your day. Even in hard seasons, His kindness shows up—in comfort, in provision, in peace. The goodness of God is not based on circumstances. It's based on His unchanging character. And He is still good.

Prayer

Lord, help me to see Your goodness today. Even when life is hard, remind me of Your faithfulness and grace.

Journal Prompt

What small sign of God's goodness have you seen lately?

My Notes & Prayers

_____

_____

_____

_____

_____

Day 45: God of the Details

Scripture

Matthew 10:29-31

Reflection

Jesus said not even a sparrow falls to the ground without the Father knowing. He knows the number of hairs on your head. That's how deeply involved God is in your life. You're not just one of many—you're seen in every detail. He's not just concerned with big-picture miracles. He's present in the everyday moments, the quiet prayers, the small needs. God of the universe is also God of your details.

Prayer

Father, thank You for caring about every part of my life. Help me trust You even in the small things today.

Journal Prompt

What detail in your life do you need to trust God with today?

My Notes & Prayers

_____

_____

_____

_____

_____

Day 46: Jesus Wept

Scripture

John 11:35

Reflection

The shortest verse in the Bible reveals something powerful—Jesus wept. He knew resurrection was coming, but still, He stopped to grieve. Jesus enters into our pain. He doesn't rush us past our sorrow. He meets us in it. Your tears are not dismissed or ignored. They are sacred to God. You don't cry alone—Jesus weeps with you.

Prayer

Jesus, thank You for entering into my sorrow. Comfort me today and remind me You are with me in my tears.

Journal Prompt

What pain do you need to bring to Jesus, knowing He weeps with you?

My Notes & Prayers

_____

_____

_____

_____

_____

Day 47: God's Timing

Scripture

Ecclesiastes 3:11

Reflection

God makes everything beautiful in its time. Not your time—His. Waiting can feel like nothing is happening, but delay is not denial. God is always working behind the scenes. He is aligning, preparing, and shaping what you cannot see. Trust His timing, even when it feels slow. His timing is never late. It's perfect—and worth the wait.

Prayer

Lord, teach me to trust Your timing. Help me wait with faith and patience, knowing You are never late.

Journal Prompt

Where do you need to release your timeline and trust God's?

My Notes & Prayers

_____

_____

_____

_____

_____

Day 48: Anchor in the Storm

📖 Scripture

Hebrews 6:19

💬 Reflection

Hope in Jesus is not wishful thinking—it's an anchor for your soul. When storms come, an anchor keeps you from drifting. It holds you steady beneath the waves. Life may shake, but you don't have to. Christ is your anchor. He is firm, secure, and unchanging. Tie your heart to Him.

🙏 Prayer

Jesus, be my anchor. When life is uncertain, help me hold tightly to You and not drift into fear.

✏️ Journal Prompt

What's been shaking you lately, and how can you anchor yourself in Christ?

✒️ My Notes & Prayers

_____

_____

_____

_____

_____

Day 49: You Are Not Forgotten

Scripture

Isaiah 49:16

Reflection

God says, "I have engraved you on the palms of My hands." That means His love permanently marks you. You are not forgotten, overlooked, or abandoned. Even when it feels silent, you are seen. Even when prayers go unanswered, you are known. God holds your name and your story close. You're never out of His heart.

Prayer

God, remind me today that I'm not forgotten. Help me rest in Your love, knowing You hold me close.

Journal Prompt

What do you need to trust today about how God sees and remembers you?

My Notes & Prayers

_____

_____

_____

_____

_____

Day 50: Faith Over Feelings

Scripture

2 Corinthians 5:7

Reflection

Feelings fluctuate, but faith is a foundation. We walk by faith, not by sight—or by emotion. This doesn't mean feelings are bad, but they're not the final authority. Faith holds onto truth even when it feels shaky. Your faith isn't based on how you think—it's based on who God is. So when feelings waver, anchor in the Word. Stand on what is eternal, not what is temporary.

Prayer

God, help me live by faith, not by how I feel. Strengthen me to trust You beyond my emotions today.

Journal Prompt

Where in your life do your feelings need to follow your faith?

My Notes & Prayers

_____

_____

_____

_____

_____

Day 51: The Power of Praise

Scripture

Psalm 100:4

Reflection

Praise is more than music—it's a weapon. It shifts your focus from problems to the presence of God. When we praise, we enter His gates. Worry lifts, hope rises, and hearts soften. You may not feel like praising, but that's often when it's most potent. Start where you are. Lift your voice. Your praise changes the atmosphere.

Prayer

Lord, fill my heart with praise today. Let worship be my response, even in challenging moments.

Journal Prompt

What can you praise God for today, even if life feels hard?

My Notes & Prayers

_____

_____

_____

_____

_____

Day 52: You're Growing

📖 Scripture

Philippians 1:6

💬 Reflection

Growth is often slow and unseen. But if God started something in you, He will finish it. You may not see the fruit yet, but that doesn't mean it's not growing. Growth happens in quiet, hidden spaces. Trust the process. Keep showing up. You are further than you think, and He is still working.

🙏 Prayer

Father, thank You for growing me even when I can't see it. Help me trust that You are completing what You began.

✏️ Journal Prompt

Where have you grown in the last season, even if it's small?

🖌️ My Notes & Prayers

_____

_____

_____

_____

_____

Day 53: Peace in the Waiting

Scripture

Isaiah 40:31

Reflection

Waiting is hard—but it's not wasted. Isaiah 40:31 says those who wait on the Lord will renew their strength. That kind of waiting isn't passive—it's hopeful, expectant, trusting. Peace doesn't mean everything is resolved. It means your heart is anchored in the One who is faithful. Let Him renew your strength as you wait. He's worth it.

Prayer

God, renew my strength in the waiting. Teach me to trust You in the in-between moments.

Journal Prompt

What are you waiting on God for, and how can you wait with peace?

My Notes & Prayers

_____

_____

_____

_____

_____

Day 54: Unshakable

Scripture

Hebrews 12:28

Reflection

Everything around us may be shaken, but the kingdom of God is unshakable. When your life is rooted in Christ, you have a firm foundation. Storms may come, but you won't be swept away. You are part of something eternal. So stand tall. Let your confidence come from what can't be shaken.

Prayer

Jesus, thank You that I am part of Your unshakable kingdom. Ground me today in Your truth and security.

Journal Prompt

What storm are you facing right now, and what truth can anchor you?

My Notes & Prayers

_____

_____

_____

_____

_____

Day 55: He Knows the Way

Scripture

Job 23:10

Reflection

When you don't understand the path, trust the One who does. Job said, 'He knows the way that I take.' Even in confusion or silence, God is still guiding. You may feel lost, but you are not abandoned. He is shaping your faith, not hiding from you. Let His knowledge of the path give you peace, even if your vision is limited.

Prayer

God, thank You for knowing the way. Help me walk in trust even when I don't see clearly.

Journal Prompt

Where do you need to lean on God's direction rather than your understanding?

My Notes & Prayers

_____

_____

_____

_____

_____

Day 56: Joy Comes in the Morning

Scripture

Psalm 30:5

Reflection

Weeping may last for a night, but joy comes in the morning. This isn't just poetic—it's a promise. Sorrow may visit, but it won't stay forever. God turns mourning into dancing, ashes into beauty. If you're in a dark season, hold on. Morning is coming. And with it, joy that only God can give.

Prayer

Lord, thank You for the promise of joy. Help me to hold on through the night and trust in Your new mercies.

Journal Prompt

What is your 'night' right now—and how can you cling to the hope of morning?

My Notes & Prayers

_____

_____

_____

_____

_____

Day 57: Refined by Fire

Scripture

1 Peter 1:6-7

Reflection

Trials test your faith—not to break it, but to refine it. Like gold in the fire, your faith is being purified. God isn't punishing you. He's strengthening you. In the heat of adversity, what's false burns away and what's eternal remains. You may not enjoy the fire, but it's producing something precious. Your faith is more valuable than gold. Let God shape it through the trial, knowing He's with you every step.

Prayer

Lord, in the middle of this trial, refine me. Strengthen my faith and help me to trust what You're doing in me.

Journal Prompt

How has a recent challenge refined your faith?

My Notes & Prayers

_____

_____

_____

_____

_____

Day 58: Carried by Grace

Scripture

Deuteronomy 1:31

Reflection

You are not walking this journey alone—God is carrying you. Like a loving Father, He lifts you when you're weak. You may not feel strong, but His grace is sustaining you. He doesn't expect you to have it all together. He invites you to lean in, rest in His arms, and let Him carry what you can't. You don't have to be enough—He already is.

Prayer

Father, carry me today. I am tired and weak, but Your grace is enough. Help me lean on You completely.

Journal Prompt

What are you carrying today that God wants to carry for you?

My Notes & Prayers

_____

_____

_____

_____

_____

Day 59: Return to Joy

Scripture

Psalm 51:12

Reflection

Joy isn't lost forever—it can be restored. David prayed for God to restore the joy of his salvation. Maybe you've been weary, distracted, or hurt. Joy may feel distant, but it's not gone. Ask God to renew it in you. He can breathe life into what feels numb. Your joy can return, not through circumstances, but through Him.

Prayer

God, restore my joy. Breathe life into places that feel dry. Let Your salvation fill my heart again with gladness.

Journal Prompt

What's one way you can return to joy today?

My Notes & Prayers

_____

_____

_____

_____

_____

Day 60: Letting Go of Control

Scripture

Proverbs 3:5-6

Reflection

You don't have to understand it all. God never asked you to carry the weight of knowing every answer. He asks you to trust Him. Letting go of control doesn't mean giving up—it means giving it to God. When you release the pressure to fix everything, you make space for peace. God is trustworthy. He is directing your path, even when it doesn't make sense.

Prayer

Lord, I surrender control. Help me trust You with every part of my journey and follow where You lead.

Journal Prompt

What area do you need to stop controlling and start trusting God with?

My Notes & Prayers

_____

_____

_____

_____

_____

Day 61: Steady in the Storm

Scripture

Mark 4:39

Reflection

Jesus didn't panic in the storm—He spoke peace to it. The disciples were afraid, but Jesus was present with them. Storms will come, but they don't define you. You can be steady because He is in your boat. Let His peace speak louder than the waves. Rest in the truth that He still calms storms.

Prayer

Jesus, speak peace over my storm. Help me remember that You are with me and I am not alone.

Journal Prompt

What's the storm in your life—and what would Jesus say to it?

My Notes & Prayers

_____

_____

_____

_____

_____

Day 62: You Are His Workmanship

Scripture

Ephesians 2:10

Reflection

You are not an accident—you are God's masterpiece. Created in Christ for good works, you were designed with purpose. Even when you feel flawed, He sees beauty. You are a part of His plan. Lean into who He made you to be. Walk in the works He prepared for you. You are His workmanship—crafted with intention and care.

Prayer

God, help me believe that I am Your masterpiece. Let me walk confidently in the purpose You created me for.

Journal Prompt

What truth about your identity do you need to believe today?

My Notes & Prayers

_____

_____

_____

_____

_____

Day 63: Rooted Deep

Scripture

Jeremiah 17:7-8

Reflection

A tree planted by water doesn't fear drought. Its roots go deep. When your roots are in God, you can endure any season. Blessed is the one who trusts in the Lord. Your strength is not in circumstances, but in where you're rooted. Stay planted in His Word. Draw from His living water. You will not wither—you will thrive.

Prayer

Lord, help me stay rooted in You. Let my faith grow deep so I can flourish in every season.

Journal Prompt

How can you deepen your spiritual roots this week?

My Notes & Prayers

_____

_____

_____

_____

_____

Day 64: Faith That Moves

Scripture

Matthew 17:20

Reflection

Faith the size of a mustard seed can move mountains. You don't need to have it all together—you just need to believe that God does. Even the smallest step in faith can shift the landscape of your life. Don't underestimate what God can do with your yes. Mountains move not by your might, but by His power. Keep believing, even if your faith feels small. God honors every bit of it.

Prayer

Lord, increase my faith. Help me to trust You with the little I have and believe You for the impossible.

Journal Prompt

What small act of faith can you take today?

My Notes & Prayers

_____

_____

_____

_____

_____

Day 65: Speak Life

Scripture

Proverbs 18:21

Reflection

Your words carry power—more than you may realize. Scripture says life and death are in the power of the tongue. What you speak matters. Are your words building up or tearing down? Are you speaking truth or fear, love or doubt? Speak life to yourself, to others, and to your future. Let your mouth agree with God's promises, not the enemy's lies.

Prayer

Jesus, help me use my words to give life today. Let what I speak reflect Your truth and love.

Journal Prompt

Who needs a life-giving word from you today?

My Notes & Prayers

_____

_____

_____

_____

_____

Day 66: More Than Enough

Scripture

2 Corinthians 9:8

Reflection

God can make all grace abound to you. That means you'll have all you need, not just barely scraping by, but overflowing. He provides not only for your survival but for your purpose. When you're aligned with Him, there is always more than enough. Lack is loud, but His provision is louder. Trust Him to meet your needs—and go beyond them.

Prayer

God, You are my provider. Help me trust in Your abundance and walk in confidence today.

Journal Prompt

Where do you need to believe God will be more than enough?

My Notes & Prayers

_____

_____

_____

_____

_____

Day 67: Forgiven and Free

Scripture

Psalm 103:12

Reflection

God has removed your sins as far as the east is from the west. That means He doesn't bring up your past—you do. When God forgives, it's complete. There's no fine print, no footnote, no shame clause. You are free. So, stop living under the condemnation that He already lifted. Walk in the freedom Jesus died to give you.

Prayer

Father, thank You for forgiveness. Help me live like I'm truly free from my past.

Journal Prompt

What guilt do you need to let go of today?

My Notes & Prayers

_____

_____

_____

_____

_____

Day 68: Living Water

Scripture

John 4:14

Reflection

Jesus offers water that never runs dry. He doesn't just quench your thirst—He becomes a well within you. Other things satisfy for a moment, but He satisfies forever. Are you running on empty? Come to the well. Drink deeply of His love, His peace, and His truth. He is your source. Stay close and stay filled.

Prayer

Jesus, I need Your living water. Fill me again with what only You can provide.

Journal Prompt

What are you turning to that doesn't satisfy?

My Notes & Prayers

_____

_____

_____

_____

_____

Day 69: Faithful in the Waiting

Scripture

Lamentations 3:25

Reflection

The Lord is good to those who wait for Him. That's hard to believe when waiting feels like silence. But God is never inactive—He's just not rushed. He works in the waiting. He builds character, grows faith, and deepens trust. Don't waste the wait. Lean in and let Him develop you there.

Prayer

God, help me to trust You in the waiting. Even when I don't see movement, remind me You are working.

Journal Prompt

How can you be faithful during your waiting season?

My Notes & Prayers

_____

_____

_____

_____

_____

Day 70: Let Your Light Shine

📖 Scripture

Matthew 5:16

💬 Reflection

You were made to shine. Not to draw attention to yourself, but to reflect God's goodness. Let your life point people to Him. Your kindness, love, and truth are light in a dark world. Don't hide it. Don't dim it. Let it shine for His glory.

🙏 Prayer

Lord, let my life reflect You. Help me shine Your light boldly and brightly today.

✍️ Journal Prompt

Where can you shine the light of Jesus today?

✍️ My Notes & Prayers

_____

_____

_____

_____

_____

Day 71: Burden Bearer

Scripture

Matthew 11:28-30

Reflection

Jesus invites the weary and burdened to come to Him, not with shame, but with trust. He offers rest for your soul, not more pressure or performance. When life feels heavy, you don't have to carry it alone. He is gentle and humble, and He understands your limits. You weren't meant to carry the world. You were meant to walk with the One who holds it. Lay it all down today. Let Him be your rest.

Prayer

Jesus, I give You the burdens I've been carrying. Teach me to rest in You and find peace for my soul.

Journal Prompt

What weight are you carrying that Jesus wants to lift?

My Notes & Prayers

_____

_____

_____

_____

_____

Day 72: You're Not Behind

Scripture

Ecclesiastes 3:1

Reflection

There is a time for everything, and that includes your journey. Comparison will convince you that you're late or lacking, but God's timing is personal. You are not behind—you are becoming. God is not rushed, and neither should you be. Trust that your story is unfolding precisely as it should. You are right where you're supposed to be.

Prayer

Lord, help me stop measuring my journey against others. Let me rest in Your perfect timing for my life.

Journal Prompt

Where do you need to release comparison and trust God's pace?

My Notes & Prayers

_____

_____

_____

_____

_____

Day 73: Even Now

Scripture

John 11:21-22

Reflection

Martha said to Jesus, 'If You had been here...' But then she added, 'Even now I know.' That's the kind of faith that believes God can still show up, even after the deadline. Even now, He can restore. Even now, He can heal. Even now, He can resurrect what feels lost. Don't stop believing because it looks too late. God is not limited by time. Your 'even now' moment may be closer than you think.

Prayer

God, I believe You can move—even now. Strengthen my faith when things seem beyond repair.

Journal Prompt

What situation feels too late, but still needs your faith?

My Notes & Prayers

_____

_____

_____

_____

_____

Day 74: God of Comfort

Scripture

2 Corinthians 1:3-4

Reflection

God doesn't just comfort you—He equips you to comfort others. His compassion is personal and purposeful. He meets you in sorrow, not just to heal you, but to help others through your story. Your pain is not wasted. Let His comfort fill you, and let it overflow. You are a vessel of hope in someone else's valley.

Prayer

Father, thank You for comforting me. Use my story to bring comfort and hope to someone else.

Journal Prompt

Who can you comfort today with the comfort you've received?

My Notes & Prayers

_____

_____

_____

_____

_____

Day 75: Chosen and Called

Scripture

1 Peter 2:9

Reflection

You are not random—you are chosen. God has called you out of darkness and into His marvelous light. That means your life has meaning. You were made to declare His praises, to reflect His light, to make a difference. Don't shrink back from your calling. You've been set apart for something sacred.

Prayer

God, thank You for choosing me. Help me walk in the calling You've placed on my life.

Journal Prompt

Where do you need to walk boldly in your calling today?

My Notes & Prayers

_____

_____

_____

_____

_____

Day 76: He Knows Your Name

Scripture

Isaiah 43:1

Reflection

God doesn't just see you—He knows you by name. That's personal, intimate, and intentional. You are not just a face in the crowd or a soul in the system. You are known. When you pass through waters, fire, or fear, He is with you. You are His. Rest in that identity today.

Prayer

Lord, thank You for calling me by name. Help me live today like I belong to You.

Journal Prompt

How does it change your day to remember that God knows you?

My Notes & Prayers

_____

_____

_____

_____

_____

Day 77: New Every Morning

Scripture

Lamentations 3:22-23

Reflection

God's mercies are not rationed—they're renewed daily. Every morning brings a fresh start, not because you earned it, but because He gives it. Yesterday's failures don't cancel today's grace. You are not stuck in your past. You are being met with new mercy today. Receive it. Walk in it. Let it define your day.

Prayer

God, thank You for Your fresh mercy. Help me receive it and begin today with hope.

Journal Prompt

What new mercy do you need to receive today?

My Notes & Prayers

_____

_____

_____

_____

_____

Day 78: Lift Up Your Eyes

Scripture

Psalm 121:1-2

Reflection

When life pulls your gaze downward, choose to lift your eyes. Your help doesn't come from within—it comes from above. God is your steady helper, your mountain mover, your ever-present help. The hills may seem high, but He is higher still. Look up. Fix your focus on the One who made heaven and earth. He won't fail you.

Prayer

God, lift my eyes today. Help me focus on Your power, not my problems.

Journal Prompt

What do you need to look up from today?

My Notes & Prayers

_____

_____

_____

_____

_____

Day 79: Seen in the Wilderness

Scripture

Exodus 3:7

Reflection

God told Moses, "I have seen the misery of My people... I have heard their cry." Before deliverance came, there was observation. God sees the wilderness. He hears your groaning. He knows. Even in delay or desert, you are not abandoned. The wilderness doesn't mean absence—it's often the place where He prepares you. Don't mistake silence for distance. Even when you don't feel Him, He sees you—and that awareness is the start of rescue.

Prayer

God, in the dry places, help me believe You still see and care. Strengthen me as I wait.

Journal Prompt

How might God be working in the background of your current wilderness?

My Notes & Prayers

_____

_____

_____

_____

_____

Day 80: All Things New

Scripture

Revelation 21:5

Reflection

God is in the business of renewal. He makes all things new, not just slightly improved or patched up. He transforms. Whatever feels worn out, broken, or hopeless in your life is not beyond His touch. His promise is restoration. You are not too far gone. Your life can still be made new.

Prayer

Jesus, I invite You to make all things new in me. Renew my heart, mind, and hope today.

Journal Prompt

What area of your life do you need Jesus to renew?

My Notes & Prayers

_____

_____

_____

_____

_____

SEASON 3

~ The 3rd 40 days ~

A season of preparation
and training.

Day 81: Guard Your Heart

Scripture

Proverbs 4:23

Reflection

Your heart is the wellspring of life—what flows from it shapes your world. That's why God says to guard it above all else. What are you allowing in? What's taking root? Tend to your heart with care. Fill it with truth, protect it from lies, and keep it soft before God.

Prayer

God, help me guard my heart today. Let it be filled with Your peace, love, and wisdom.

Journal Prompt

What boundary do you need to set to guard your heart better?

My Notes & Prayers

_____

_____

_____

_____

_____

Day 82: He Is With You

Scripture

Joshua 1:9

Reflection

Courage isn't the absence of fear—it's choosing faith in the face of fear. God told Joshua to be strong and courageous, not because he had all the answers, but because God was with him. That's your reason, too. Whatever you face today, you do not face it alone. God goes before you and stays beside you. Be bold. He's got you.

Prayer

Father, give me courage today. Remind me that I am never alone—you are with me always.

Journal Prompt

What step of courage can you take today, knowing God is with you?

My Notes & Prayers

_____

_____

_____

_____

_____

Day 83: Unfailing Love

Scripture

Psalm 33:22

Reflection

The love of God never runs out, wears out, or fades away. It's not based on your performance—it's rooted in His character. When you feel unworthy, His love remains. When you've failed, His love is steadfast. Let His love be your security today. You are loved, and that won't change.

Prayer

God, help me rest in Your unfailing love. Let it be the foundation of my identity today.

Journal Prompt

How can you live today more rooted in God's love than others' approval?

My Notes & Prayers

_____

_____

_____

_____

_____

Day 84: Freedom in Truth

Scripture

John 8:32

Reflection

Truth isn't just knowledge—it's freedom. Jesus said the truth will set you free. That means the lies you believe are chains. When you live by His truth, you walk in freedom. What truth do you need to reclaim today? God's Word is not just informative—it's liberating.

Prayer

Jesus, reveal any lie I've believed. Help me replace it with Your truth and walk in freedom.

Journal Prompt

What truth from God's Word do you need to hold onto right now?

My Notes & Prayers

_____

_____

_____

_____

_____

Day 85: The God Who Hears

Scripture

Psalm 34:17

Reflection

When the righteous cry for help, the Lord hears and delivers them. This is your assurance—God hears you. Not one cry, sigh, or whisper goes unnoticed. Even when you feel like your prayers bounce off the ceiling, He is listening. He is not far off or indifferent. He is close, attentive, and faithful to respond in His perfect way. Keep praying, keep believing—He hears you now.

Prayer

God, thank You for hearing me. Even when I don't see the answer yet, I trust that You are listening and working.

Journal Prompt

What prayer do you need to pray again, trusting that God hears?

My Notes & Prayers

_____

_____

_____

_____

_____

Day 86: Light in the Darkness

Scripture

John 1:5

Reflection

The light shines in the darkness, and the darkness has not overcome it. No matter how dark things seem, light wins. Jesus, is that light. He shines into your fears, failures, and confusion, not to expose and shame, but to guide and heal. Darkness can't extinguish what He brings. Let Him light your path today.

Prayer

Jesus, shine Your light in every area of my life. Let darkness flee and hope rise in me.

Journal Prompt

What dark place in your life needs the light of Jesus?

My Notes & Prayers

_____

_____

_____

_____

_____

Day 87: Secure in His Hands

📖 Scripture

John 10:28-29

💬 Reflection

You are held securely in the hands of Jesus, and nothing can snatch you away. That's not conditional or fragile—it's guaranteed. When you feel unstable, unsure, or afraid, remember who holds you. You are not alone, not lost, not slipping through the cracks. You are safe in His hands.

🙏 Prayer

God, thank You for holding me. Even when I waver, Your grip on me is firm. Let me rest in that security today.

✏️ Journal Prompt

How can you live today with confidence that God holds you?

📝 My Notes & Prayers

_____

_____

_____

_____

_____

Day 88: Content in Christ

Scripture

Philippians 4:11-13

Reflection

Contentment isn't about having everything—it's about knowing you already have what matters most. Paul learned to be content in any situation because his strength was Christ. You can do the same. Whether in plenty or in lack, joy or hardship, you are not without strength. Christ is your constant. Lean into Him, and you will find contentment beyond circumstance.

Prayer

Jesus, teach me to be content in You. Help me rely on Your strength in every season.

Journal Prompt

What area of your life do you need to stop striving and start trusting?

My Notes & Prayers

_____

_____

_____

_____

_____

Day 89: He Makes a Way

📖 Scripture

Isaiah 43:19

💬 Reflection

God makes a way where there seems to be no way. In the wilderness, in the wasteland, in the places where hope feels dry—He is doing a new thing. You may not see it yet, but He is working. He's not limited by what's logical or predictable. He is a Way Maker. Trust Him to open doors you didn't know existed.

🙏 Prayer

Lord, make a way in my life. Show me where You're moving and help me walk forward in faith.

✏️ Journal Prompt

What situation do you need to trust God to make a way through?

🖊 My Notes & Prayers

_____

_____

_____

_____

_____

Day 90: Joy Comes in the Morning

Scripture

Psalm 30:5

Reflection

Weeping may last for the night, but joy comes in the morning. Your sorrow is not permanent. The night will not last forever. God has a sunrise of hope prepared for you. Don't lose heart—joy is on the horizon. Hold on. The morning is coming.

Prayer

Father, give me hope for the morning. Let joy rise in me, even in the middle of my night.

Journal Prompt

What sorrow do you need to surrender while you wait for joy?

My Notes & Prayers

_____

_____

_____

_____

_____

Day 91: Never Forsaken

Scripture

Hebrews 13:5

Reflection

God has promised never to leave or forsake you. That's not based on your performance—it's anchored in His love. When others walk away, He stays. When you feel alone, He is still present. You are never abandoned. You are held, seen, and deeply loved. Let that truth settle your heart today.

Prayer

Jesus, thank You for never leaving me. Help me feel Your nearness in every moment.

Journal Prompt

When have you felt forsaken—and how is God reminding you He's still there?

My Notes & Prayers

_____

_____

_____

_____

_____

Day 92: Grace That Covers

Scripture

Romans 5:20

Reflection

Where sin increased, grace abounded all the more. That means your failures don't disqualify you—they draw God's grace near. His grace doesn't run out, and it doesn't give up. It covers, cleanses, and restores. You don't need to earn your way back. You need only receive what He freely gives. Let grace cover the places shame has tried to define.

Prayer

Jesus, thank You for Your grace that goes beyond my failures. Help me live today covered in Your mercy and truth.

Journal Prompt

What area of your life needs to be covered in grace today?

My Notes & Prayers

_____

_____

_____

_____

_____

Day 93: You Belong

Scripture

Ephesians 2:19

Reflection

You are no longer a stranger or outsider—you belong in God's family. In Christ, you are accepted, valued, and seen. You don't have to fight for your place or prove your worth. You have already been chosen. Let that truth settle deep in your soul. You're not on the outside looking in—you're home.

Prayer

God, thank You for calling me Your child. Let me live today with confidence that I belong to You.

Journal Prompt

Where in your life do you need to embrace your identity as God's beloved?

My Notes & Prayers

_____

_____

_____

_____

_____

Day 94: He Leads You

Scripture

Psalm 23:2-3

Reflection

God doesn't just save you—He leads you. He brings you to still waters and restores your soul. He doesn't drive you with fear but leads you with love. You can follow Him without hesitation. Even when you can't see the whole path, trust the Shepherd. He knows the way—and He walks with you.

Prayer

Jesus, be my Shepherd today. Lead me in peace and help me trust Your direction.

Journal Prompt

What area of your life do you need to surrender to God's leadership?

My Notes & Prayers

_____

_____

_____

_____

_____

Day 95: Nothing Can Separate

Scripture

Romans 8:38-39

Reflection

There is nothing—absolutely nothing—that can separate you from the love of God. Not your past, not your pain, not your doubts. His love is unshakable, unstoppable, and unconditional. When you feel distant, remember: He hasn't moved. He's still holding you. Still choosing you. Still loving you fiercely and faithfully.

Prayer

God, thank You that nothing can separate me from Your love. Let that truth quiet every fear in me today.

Journal Prompt

What lie are you believing that contradicts God's unshakable love?

My Notes & Prayers

_____   _____

_____

_____   _____

_____

_____

Day 96: Peace in the Storm

📖 Scripture

Mark 4:39

💬 Reflection

Jesus calmed the storm with a word—and He still does. Storms will come, but they don't get the final say. Jesus is your peace, even when the waves rise. He doesn't just bring calm—He is calm. Invite Him into your fear, and watch the storm lose its power.

🙏 Prayer

Lord, speak peace over my heart today. Help me trust You even when everything feels chaotic.

✏️ Journal Prompt

What storm in your life needs to hear Jesus say, 'Peace, be still'?

🖌️ My Notes & Prayers

_____

_____

_____

_____

_____

Day 97: His Strength in You

Scripture

2 Corinthians 12:9

Reflection

God's strength is made perfect in your weakness. That's not a reason to hide your struggles—it's a reason to lean in. When you are weak, He is strong. You don't have to be enough—He already is. Let His grace carry what you cannot. There's power in surrender.

Prayer

God, I surrender my weakness to You today. Let Your strength be what sustains me.

Journal Prompt

Where do you need to stop striving and start surrendering?

My Notes & Prayers

_____

_____

_____

_____

_____

Day 98: Run the Race

Scripture

Hebrews 12:1-2

Reflection

You are in a race, not to compete, but to finish faithfully. Throw off the weights that slow you down. Fix your eyes on Jesus. Run with endurance, not because it's easy, but because He is worth it. You're not running alone. He is with you every step.

Prayer

Jesus, help me run my race today. Keep my focus on You and give me the strength to keep going.

Journal Prompt

What's one weight you can lay down so you can run lighter?

My Notes & Prayers

_____

_____

_____

_____

_____

Day 99: Trust the Process

Scripture

Philippians 1:6

Reflection

God began a good work in you, and He will carry it to completion. You may not see the progress you want, but God is not finished. Transformation takes time. Healing takes time. Trust the process—even the slow, silent parts. God wastes nothing. Every step forward, every setback, is part of His plan to make you whole.

Prayer

Lord, help me trust that You are still working, even when I don't see it. Finish the good work You've started in me.

Journal Prompt

What unfinished area in your life do you need to entrust to God today?

My Notes & Prayers

_____

_____

_____

_____

_____

Day 100: Rooted in Love

Scripture

Ephesians 3:17-18

Reflection

You are rooted and grounded in love, not performance, not fear, not success. God's love is the soil that stabilizes your soul. When life tries to shake you, go deeper into His love. It's wide enough for every failure and long enough for every journey. You are held and nourished in His love.

Prayer

Father, root me deeper in Your love today. Let it be the foundation I stand on and the source I draw from.

Journal Prompt

What truth about God's love do you need to re-root yourself in today?

My Notes & Prayers

_____

_____

_____

_____

_____

Day 101: Steady in the Waiting

Scripture

Isaiah 40:31

Reflection

Waiting isn't wasted when it's placed in God's hands. Those who wait on the Lord renew their strength—not just endure, but rise. In the waiting, He's strengthening you, preparing you, and anchoring your hope. Don't rush ahead. Wait well. Soar in His timing, not your own.

Prayer

God, teach me to wait well. Let my strength be renewed as I place my hope in You.

Journal Prompt

Where in your life do you need to stop striving and start waiting?

My Notes & Prayers

_____

_____

_____

_____

_____

Day 102: He's Still in Control

Scripture

Colossians 1:17

Reflection

In Him all things hold together. That includes your life. When everything feels like it's falling apart, remember who holds it all. Jesus is not panicked. He's not confused or distant. He is sovereign, steady, and holding you together with His hands of grace.

Prayer

Jesus, hold me together today. Remind me that You are in control and I am secure in You.

Journal Prompt

What part of your life do you need to entrust again to God's control?

My Notes & Prayers

_____

_____

_____

_____

_____

Day 103: Speak Life

Scripture

Proverbs 18:21

Reflection

Your words carry weight—power to build or break. Choose life-giving speech today. Speak hope to yourself. Speak encouragement to others. Speak truth over your circumstances. Don't underestimate the power of one word spoken in faith. Let your mouth be a well of life.

Prayer

Lord, help me guard my words today. Let my speech reflect Your grace, truth, and love.

Journal Prompt

What do you need to speak differently—over yourself or someone else?

My Notes & Prayers

_____

_____

_____

_____

_____

Day 104: He Knows What You Need

Scripture

Matthew 6:8

Reflection

Before you even ask, your Father knows what you need. That's not just knowledge—it's care. He is not unaware of your needs or dismissive of your heart. He sees, He knows, and He provides in ways beyond what you expect. Come to Him today—not to inform, but to trust.

Prayer

God, thank You for knowing my needs before I speak them. Help me rest in Your provision and trust Your timing.

Journal Prompt

Where do you need to stop worrying and start trusting in God's care?

My Notes & Prayers

_____

_____

_____

_____

_____

Day 105: Forgiven and Free

Scripture

1 John 1:9

Reflection

If we confess our sins, He is faithful and just to forgive. There is no delay, no loophole—just mercy. You are not too far gone. You are not too broken. His forgiveness frees you from shame and restores you to a relationship. Walk in that freedom today.

Prayer

Jesus, thank You for forgiving me. Help me walk in the freedom that only You provide.

Journal Prompt

What do you need to bring into the light so you can live free?

My Notes & Prayers

_____

_____

_____

_____

_____

Day 106: He Carries You

Scripture

Isaiah 46:4

Reflection

From birth to old age, God promises to carry you. You don't have to carry everything on your shoulders. When the weight is too heavy, He lifts it. When your strength is gone, His strength takes over. There is never a moment when He sets you down. Let yourself be carried today.

Prayer

Lord, carry me today. Lift what I cannot handle and remind me You are always with me.

Journal Prompt

What burden do you need to hand over to God today?

My Notes & Prayers

_____

_____

_____

_____

_____

Day 107: Draw Near

Scripture

James 4:8

Reflection

Draw near to God, and He will draw near to you. This is an open invitation to closeness with your Creator. You don't need to perform, perfect, or pretend—just come. God desires your nearness. Even a whisper is enough. He's waiting with open arms.

Prayer

Father, I draw near to You. Pull me close and let me feel Your presence again.

Journal Prompt

How can you create space today to draw near to God?

My Notes & Prayers

_____

_____

_____

_____

_____

Day 108: In the Waiting

Scripture

Lamentations 3:25

Reflection

The Lord is good to those who wait for Him. Waiting is not passive—it's an act of trust. When you wait, you declare God is worth the time. He's not in a rush, and His timing is never wrong. Trust Him in the waiting. Even silence is sacred when He is near.

Prayer

God, help me wait on You with patience and expectation. Let my hope rise in the quiet moments.

Journal Prompt

What does waiting well look like for you today?

My Notes & Prayers

_____

_____

_____

_____

_____

Day 109: Joy in the Journey

Scripture

1 Thessalonians 5:16

Reflection

Rejoice always. Not because everything is good, but because God is always good. Joy is not based on circumstances—it's rooted in Christ. You can have joy in sorrow, peace in chaos, and hope in hardship. Look for joy today, and you'll find Him in the midst of it.

Prayer

Jesus, give me joy today that surpasses my situation. Let my heart rejoice in Your goodness.

Journal Prompt

What's one thing you can be grateful for today, even in difficulty?

My Notes & Prayers

_____

_____

_____

_____

_____

Day 110: His Ways Are Higher

Scripture

Isaiah 55:8-9

Reflection

God's thoughts are not your thoughts, and His ways are far beyond yours. You won't always understand what He's doing—but you can always trust Him. When the road doesn't make sense, walk it anyway. He sees the end from the beginning. He is not just writing your story—He's weaving it into eternity.

Prayer

Lord, help me trust Your ways, even when they're not mine. Give me faith to follow when I don't understand.

Journal Prompt

Where do you need to let go of understanding and trust God instead?

My Notes & Prayers

_____

_____

_____

_____

_____

Day 111: You Are Seen

Scripture

Luke 12:6-7

Reflection

Not even a sparrow falls without God noticing, and you are worth more than many sparrows. God knows the number of hairs on your head. He sees every detail, every tear, every sigh. You are not invisible. You are fully known and deeply seen. You matter more than you know.

Prayer

Father, thank You for seeing me. Help me live with confidence that I am known and loved.

Journal Prompt

When have you felt unseen—and how does God speak into that today?

My Notes & Prayers

_____

_____

_____

_____

_____

Day 112: He Redeems Everything

Scripture

Joel 2:25

Reflection

God promises to restore what the locusts have eaten. Nothing is too lost for Him to redeem. Your pain is not wasted. Your past is not beyond His repair. He restores time, relationships, and broken dreams. What feels ruined can become radiant in His hands.

Prayer

Redeemer, bring restoration to the broken areas of my life. Show me Your beauty in the places that feel barren.

Journal Prompt

What's one area you're praying God will redeem in your life?

My Notes & Prayers

_____

_____

_____

_____

_____

Day 113: Strong When You're Weak

Scripture

2 Corinthians 12:10

Reflection

Paul said he delighted in weaknesses because when he was weak, then he was strong. This is the paradox of grace—your lowest moments are where God's strength is most visible. Don't hide your weakness. Let it be a place where God's power rests. He is not asking for your perfection—He's asking for your surrender. Let Him be strong in you today.

Prayer

God, I surrender my weakness to You. Let Your power be made perfect in my imperfection.

Journal Prompt

Where have you felt weak, and how might God want to show His strength there?

My Notes & Prayers

_____

_____

_____

_____

_____

Day 114: He is With You

Scripture

Joshua 1:9

Reflection

Be strong and courageous—not because you're fearless, but because God is with you. That's your confidence: not in your own strength, but in His unshakable presence. Wherever you go, whatever you face, He goes with you. Let that truth breathe courage into your soul.

Prayer

Lord, help me be brave today—not because I'm strong, but because You are near.

Journal Prompt

What decision or situation do you need to face with God's courage today?

My Notes & Prayers

_____

_____

_____

_____

_____

Day 115: Faith That Endures

Scripture

James 1:12

Reflection

Blessed is the one who remains steadfast under trial. Endurance isn't glamorous, but it's powerful. When you keep showing up, keep trusting, and keep holding on, God honors that. He strengthens your roots and deepens your faith. Let perseverance have its work in you today—you are becoming stronger than you know.

Prayer

God, give me endurance today. Help me stay faithful, even when it's hard.

Journal Prompt

What challenge are you enduring—and how has it shaped your faith?

My Notes & Prayers

_____

_____

_____

_____

_____

Day 116: Grace for Today

Scripture

Matthew 6:34

Reflection

Don't worry about tomorrow—today has enough grace for what you face. God isn't asking you to carry future burdens. He's giving you strength for this day, this moment, this breath. Focus on what's in front of you. Grace will meet you in real time.

Prayer

Lord, give me grace for today. Help me live in the present and trust You with the rest.

Journal Prompt

What worry do you need to release so you can live today fully?

My Notes & Prayers

_____

_____

_____

_____

_____

Day 117: Unshaken

Scripture

Psalm 16:8

Reflection

I have set the Lord always before me; because He is at my right hand, I will not be shaken. When your focus is on God, fear loses its grip. He stabilizes your soul. Storms may come, but your foundation is firm. Set your eyes on Him today—and find your footing.

Prayer

Jesus, be my anchor today. Keep me steady and secure in Your presence.

Journal Prompt

What fear or distraction do you need to refocus back on God?

My Notes & Prayers

_____

_____

_____

_____

_____

Day 118: Let Go and Let God

Scripture

Proverbs 3:5-6

Reflection

Trust in the Lord with all your heart and lean not on your own understanding. There's freedom in surrender. You don't have to figure everything out. God knows the path, even when you don't. Let go of control and let Him lead you today.

Prayer

God, I choose to trust You. Lead me in the way I should go, even when I don't understand.

Journal Prompt

What decision are you trying to control instead of trusting God with?

My Notes & Prayers

_____

_____

_____

_____

_____

Day 119: Hope That Anchors

Scripture

Hebrews 6:19

Reflection

We have this hope as an anchor for the soul, firm and secure. Hope isn't wishful thinking—it's confident expectation in God's promises. When life feels unstable, let hope ground you. You are not drifting—you are anchored. God is not finished yet.

Prayer

Lord, be the anchor of my soul today. Secure me in Your truth and give me hope that holds firm.

Journal Prompt

What promise of God do you need to hold onto right now?

My Notes & Prayers

_____

_____

_____

_____

_____

Day 120: Keep Showing Up

Scripture

Galatians 6:9

Reflection

Don't grow weary in doing good. You may not see the fruit yet, but it's growing. God honors the small acts of faithfulness. Keep praying, keep trusting, keep showing up. In due time, you will reap—He promised. Your consistency is not in vain.

Prayer

Lord, help me not to give up. Give me endurance to keep walking in obedience today.

Journal Prompt

Where do you need to keep sowing, even when you feel weary?

My Notes & Prayers

_____

_____

_____

_____

_____

SEASON 4

~ The 4th 40 days ~

A season of new life and victory.

Day 121: Your Story Isn't Over

Scripture

Philippians 1:6

Reflection

God finishes what He starts. That means your story is still unfolding.
You may be in a chapter of pain or confusion, but it's not the final
word. Trust the Author. He's writing redemption through every line.
Your story is in good hands.

Prayer

Jesus, write Your story through my life. Help me trust the process
even when I don't see the whole picture.

Journal Prompt

What unfinished place in your life do you need to trust God with?

My Notes & Prayers

_____

_____

_____

_____

_____

Day 122: Freedom in Forgiveness

Scripture

Matthew 6:14

Reflection

Forgiveness isn't about forgetting—it's about freeing. When you release others, you release yourself from bitterness. God has forgiven you; let that fuel the grace you extend. It may not be easy, but it's freeing. Forgiveness unlocks the door to peace.

Prayer

Father, help me forgive as You have forgiven me. Give me the courage to release what I've been holding.

Journal Prompt

Who do you need to forgive to find freedom?

My Notes & Prayers

_____

_____

_____

_____

_____

Day 123: God is Still Good

Scripture

Nahum 1:7

Reflection

The Lord is good, a refuge in times of trouble. Even when life isn't good, God is. His goodness isn't based on outcomes—it's based on who He is. Let your anchor be in His nature, not your circumstances. He is faithful, even now.

Prayer

God, remind me today that You are good. Help me trust Your heart, even in the most challenging times.

Journal Prompt

What situation feels hard, and how can you remind yourself of God's goodness?

My Notes & Prayers

_____

_____

_____

_____

_____

Day 124: Clothed in Strength

📖 Scripture

Proverbs 31:25

💬 Reflection

She is clothed with strength and dignity. This isn't about perfection—it's about divine empowerment. God has covered you in strength for what lies ahead. You don't need to strive for worth—you wear it. Stand tall today in the identity He's given you.

🙏 Prayer

Lord, dress me in Your strength today. Help me face this day with dignity and courage.

📝 Journal Prompt

What area of your life do you need to walk in strength and dignity?

✍️ My Notes & Prayers

_____

_____

_____

_____

Day 125: Faith Over Fear

Scripture

2 Timothy 1:7

Reflection

God has not given you a spirit of fear. So when fear rises, remember it's not from Him. You've been given power, love, and a sound mind. Stand firm in faith. Choose belief over anxiety. Walk today in holy confidence.

Prayer

God, replace my fear with faith. Let Your Spirit lead me in power and peace.

Journal Prompt

What fear are you facing—and how can faith lead you through it?

My Notes & Prayers

_____

_____

_____

_____

_____

Day 126: You're Never Alone

Scripture

Deuteronomy 31:6

Reflection

God will never leave you or forsake you. That's a promise, not a feeling. When you feel alone, you aren't. He is right there—in the silence, in the tears, in the unknown. You are always held, always seen, always loved.

Prayer

Jesus, remind me today that I am never alone. Be near and let me feel Your presence.

Journal Prompt

Where do you need to remember that God is with you?

My Notes & Prayers

_____

_____

_____

_____

_____

Day 127: Overflowing Grace

Scripture

2 Corinthians 9:8

Reflection

God can bless you abundantly so that in all things at all times, you have all that you need. Grace is not just enough—it overflows. You're not meant to live in scarcity when His grace is abundant. Lean into that grace today. Let it fill your empty spaces and spill into the lives around you.

Prayer

Lord, let Your grace overflow in me today. Help me to receive and reflect Your abundance.

Journal Prompt

Where do you need to receive God's grace more fully today?

My Notes & Prayers

_____

_____

_____

_____

_____

Day 128: He Delights in You

Scripture

Zephaniah 3:17

Reflection

God rejoices over you with singing. He doesn't just tolerate you—He delights in you. You are not a burden. You are not invisible. You are the joy of His heart. Rest in His affection today. Let it silence your self-doubt and speak peace to your soul.

Prayer

Father, help me believe that You delight in me. Let Your love quiet my heart and lift my spirit.

Journal Prompt

How would your day change if you lived like God truly delighted in you?

My Notes & Prayers

_____

_____

_____

_____

_____

Day 129: The Lord Will Fight For You

📖 Scripture

Exodus 14:14

💬 Reflection

You don't have to fight every battle on your own. Sometimes the most faithful thing you can do is be still. God is your defender, your protector, your strength. When the enemy comes in like a flood, the Lord raises a standard. Let Him fight for you today. He never loses a battle.

🙏 Prayer

God, I give You my battles today. Help me rest in the truth that You fight for me.

✏️ Journal Prompt

What fight do you need to surrender to God's hands today?

✍️ My Notes & Prayers

_____

_____

_____

_____

_____

Day 130: From Ashes to Beauty

📖 Scripture

Isaiah 61:3

💬 Reflection

God gives beauty for ashes. He doesn't discard what's broken—He transforms it. Whatever ashes you hold—grief, loss, regret—place them in His hands. Watch Him turn sorrow into joy, mourning into dancing. His restoration is real. Believe again in beauty.

🙏 Prayer

Jesus, I give You my ashes. Bring beauty where there has been only loss.

✏️ Journal Prompt

What ashes in your life need to be surrendered for God's beauty to rise?

✍️ My Notes & Prayers

_____

_____

_____

_____

_____

Day 131: Peace Beyond Understanding

Scripture

Philippians 4:7

Reflection

The peace of God surpasses all understanding. It's not the kind of peace that makes sense—it's deeper. It guards your heart and mind like a fortress. When everything feels out of control, His peace anchors you. You don't have to understand to rest. You just have to receive.

Prayer

Lord, let Your peace guard my mind today. Still my anxious heart and center me in You.

Journal Prompt

Where do you need peace today, even if your situation hasn't changed?

My Notes & Prayers

_____

_____

_____

_____

_____

Day 132: Faith Like a Mustard Seed

Scripture

Matthew 17:20

Reflection

Even the smallest faith can move mountains. You don't need perfect faith—you need planted faith. God honors what you're willing to give Him. So offer your mustard seed. Believe again. Speak again. Move forward in faith and watch Him work.

Prayer

Jesus, I give You the little faith I have. Grow it and move in my life in mighty ways.

Journal Prompt

What small step of faith can you take today?

My Notes & Prayers

_____

_____

_____

_____

_____

Day 133: You Are His Workmanship

Scripture

Ephesians 2:10

Reflection

You are God's workmanship—His masterpiece. You were created with intention and purpose. You're not a mistake or an afterthought. You are made for good works that God prepared in advance. Walk boldly in that purpose today. He is shaping you for something beautiful.

Prayer

God, help me believe that I am Your workmanship. Let me walk with purpose and confidence today.

Journal Prompt

What step can you take to live out the purpose God has placed in you?

My Notes & Prayers

_____

_____

_____

_____

_____

Day 134: Planted, Not Buried

📖 Scripture

John 12:24

💬 Reflection

Unless a seed falls to the ground and dies, it remains alone. But if it dies, it bears much fruit. What feels like a burial may be planting. God uses seasons of obscurity to grow something new in you. Trust that your unseen obedience is preparing something fruitful.

🙏 Prayer

Lord, help me trust that the quiet seasons are not wasted. Use what feels hidden to grow something eternal in me.

✏️ Journal Prompt

What feels buried that might actually be planted in this season?

🖌️ My Notes & Prayers

_____

_____

_____

_____

_____

Day 135: He Restores My Soul

Scripture

Psalm 23:3

Reflection

He restores your soul. When your heart is weary, when your strength is gone—He brings you back to life. God doesn't just heal symptoms. He restores the depths of your being. Let Him shepherd you gently today and breathe rest into your soul.

Prayer

Shepherd, lead me beside still waters today. Restore what's been worn down in me.

Journal Prompt

Where do you feel weary and in need of soul-restoration?

My Notes & Prayers

_____

_____

_____

_____

_____

Day 136: Secure in His Hands

Scripture

John 10:28

Reflection

Jesus said no one can snatch you out of His hand. That's security. No matter what shakes around you, you are safe in Him. Your salvation is not fragile. Rest in the strength of His grip. He holds you tightly and lovingly.

Prayer

Jesus, thank You that I'm secure in You. Help me trust that nothing can separate me from Your love.

Journal Prompt

What fear can you surrender because you know God is holding you?

My Notes & Prayers

_____

_____

_____

_____

Day 137: Light for the Path Ahead

Scripture

Psalm 119:105 – "Your word is a lamp to my feet and a light to my path."

Reflection

Life can sometimes feel like walking through a tunnel without knowing when the light will come. But God's Word isn't just a distant beacon—it's a lamp at your feet. It doesn't always illuminate the entire road, but it gives enough light for the next faithful step. His truth pushes back the fog of fear, confusion, and doubt. You don't have to see the whole picture to move forward. You only need to trust the One who walks with you. When uncertainty clouds your mind, lean into His promises. They will not fail you. And when darkness seems loud, remember: even the smallest flame still defeats the night.

Prayer

God, when I can't see what's next, help me follow the light of Your Word. Thank You for guiding my steps with truth, even when the road ahead feels unclear.

Journal Prompt

What small step of faith can you take today by trusting God's Word to lead you?

My Notes & Prayers

_____

_____

_____

_____

_____

Day 138: Named with Purpose

Scripture

Isaiah 43:1 – "Do not fear, for I have redeemed you; I have called you by name; you are Mine."

Reflection

You're not just known—you're named. That means God doesn't simply recognize you from afar. He speaks your name with purpose, affection, and calling. In a world where labels are thrown around—success, failure, not enough—God interrupts with something different: Mine. His naming speaks of redemption, belonging, and destiny. Even when you forget who you are, He doesn't. He formed you with intention and calls you into identity, not performance. The world may define you by your past or your role, but the One who created you defines you by your worth. Let that name—His—be the loudest one you hear today.

Prayer

Father, thank You for naming me and calling me Your own. Drown out the lies I've believed and help me live from the truth of who I am in You.

Journal Prompt

What false names or labels have you been living under—and what does God call you instead?

My Notes & Prayers

_____

_____

_____

_____

_____

Day 139: Still Waters, Deep Peace

Scripture

Psalm 23:2

Reflection

He leads you beside still waters. Not chaotic ones—still. God wants to quiet your soul and speak peace into your storm. Let Him lead you today. Follow Him to calm, to clarity, to peace that passes understanding.

Prayer

Jesus, guide me to still waters. Let me hear Your voice above the noise.

Journal Prompt

Where is God calling you to slow down and receive His peace?

My Notes & Prayers

_____

_____

_____

_____

_____

Day 140: Faithful in the Fire

Scripture

Daniel 3:25

Reflection

Even in the fire, God is with you. Shadrach, Meshach, and Abednego walked in the flames, but they were not alone. God didn't prevent the fire, but He showed up in it. He does the same for you. Whatever you face, His presence changes everything.

Prayer

Lord, even in the heat of trial, let me feel Your nearness. Thank You for being with me in every fire.

Journal Prompt

What 'fire' are you in right now, and how can you sense God's presence in it?

My Notes & Prayers

_____

_____

_____

_____

_____

Day 141: Come As You Are

Scripture

Matthew 11:28

Reflection

Jesus doesn't ask you to clean yourself up before coming to Him. He simply says, 'Come.' With your burdens, your exhaustion, your mess, He welcomes you as you are. This is the grace of the Gospel: we don't earn our way to rest, we receive it. Let Him carry what's weighing you down today. He is gentle with your soul.

Prayer

Jesus, I come to You just as I am. Take my weariness and give me Your rest.

Journal Prompt

What burden are you carrying today that you need to hand to Jesus?

My Notes & Prayers

_____

_____

_____

_____

_____

Day 142: Steady in the Storm

Scripture

Mark 4:39

Reflection

When the storm raged, Jesus spoke peace. That same voice still speaks to your storms today. He doesn't promise calm circumstances—but He promises His presence and peace. You can stand steady when the wind howls because the Prince of Peace is in your boat. Let His words settle your heart today.

Prayer

Lord, speak peace over my fears. Help me trust You in the middle of the storm.

Journal Prompt

What storm in your life needs to hear the calming voice of Jesus?

My Notes & Prayers

_____

_____

_____

_____

_____

Day 143: The Gift of Today

Scripture

Psalm 118:24

Reflection

This is the day the Lord has made—rejoice and be glad. Not because everything is perfect, but because it's a gift. Today is sacred. It's full of divine opportunities, small joys, and unseen miracles. Don't rush past it. Savor what God has placed in front of you.

Prayer

God, thank You for this day. Help me live it fully and gratefully.

Journal Prompt

What small blessings can you rejoice in today?

My Notes & Prayers

_____

_____

_____

_____

_____

Day 144: When You Feel Forgotten

Scripture

Isaiah 49:15-16

Reflection

God says, 'I will not forget you. I have engraved you on the palms of my hands.' Even when people overlook or abandon you, He never will. You are deeply known, intimately seen, and eternally loved. You are not forgotten. You are carved into the hands of the One who holds the world.

Prayer

Father, remind me that I am never out of Your sight. Even when I feel forgotten, help me feel Your nearness.

Journal Prompt

What truth about God's care can anchor you when you feel overlooked?

My Notes & Prayers

_____

_____

_____

_____

_____

Day 145: Faith to Begin Again

Scripture

Lamentations 3:22-23

Reflection

God's mercies are new every morning. Every sunrise is an invitation to begin again. No matter what yesterday held, grace meets you today. You are not stuck. God is the God of fresh starts and restored hope. Take one faithful step forward today.

Prayer

Lord, thank You for Your new mercies today. Give me the courage to begin again.

Journal Prompt

Where in your life do you need to begin again with God's mercy?

My Notes & Prayers

_____

_____

_____

_____

_____

Day 146: Unseen But Known

Scripture

Luke 12:7

Reflection

Even the hairs on your head are numbered. That's how detailed God's love is. You may feel overlooked by the world, but God fully knows you. Nothing about you is insignificant to Him. Let that truth ground you when insecurity rises.

Prayer

Jesus, thank You for knowing me completely and loving me fully. Anchor my worth in You.

Journal Prompt

What part of your identity needs to be rooted in God's knowledge of you?

My Notes & Prayers

_____

_____

_____

_____

_____

Day 147: Fill Me With Living Water

Scripture

John 4:14

Reflection

Jesus offers water that quenches the soul's thirst. Nothing else will satisfy—not success, approval, or distraction. He alone fills the empty spaces. Drink deeply of His truth today. Let His presence refresh your soul.

Prayer

Lord, I come thirsty. Fill me with living water that only You can give.

Journal Prompt

What are you seeking that only Jesus can truly satisfy?

My Notes & Prayers

_____

_____

_____

_____

_____

Day 148: You're Not Just Seen—You're Sought

Scripture

Genesis 16:13

Reflection

When Hagar fled in fear, God didn't just see her—He **found** her. That's the heart of El Roi, the God who sees: not just watching, but pursuing. God doesn't wait for you to get it together—He seeks you out in your lowest, loneliest moments. His seeing leads to action. He meets you where you are and speaks truth over the lies you've believed. In every moment you've wanted to disappear, God came looking. His seeing means rescue, restoration, and redirection.

Prayer

Lord, thank You for seeking me, not just seeing me. Help me receive Your pursuit and respond in trust.

Journal Prompt

When has God found you in a hard place and spoken life into your situation?

My Notes & Prayers

_____

_____

_____

_____

_____

Day 149: Refined, Not Ruined

Scripture

1 Peter 1:7

Reflection

Trials refine your faith like fire refines gold. They don't ruin you—they purify you. Pain has purpose in the hands of God. What feels like breaking may actually be shaping. Let your trials turn you toward trust, not despair.

Prayer

Lord, in my trials, refine me. Help me see how You are strengthening my faith.

Journal Prompt

What trial are you facing—and what might God be refining in you?

My Notes & Prayers

_____

_____

_____

_____

_____

Day 150: An Ever-Present Help

Scripture

Psalm 46:1

Reflection

God is your refuge and strength, a very present help in trouble. He's not distant or delayed—He's present. In your chaos, He's near. In your fear, He's faithful. You're not facing this alone. You're walking with the God who holds all things together.

Prayer

God, be my refuge today. Remind me that You are with me right here and right now.

Journal Prompt

What challenge are you walking through—and how can you draw on God's nearness?

My Notes & Prayers

_____

_____

_____

_____

_____

Day 151: Perfect Love Casts Out Fear

Scripture

1 John 4:18

Reflection

Where there is perfect love, fear can't stay. God's love is not conditional or partial—it's complete. Let His love surround you and silence fear. You are safe in His care. Let go of the what-ifs and rest in the I AM.

Prayer

Father, fill me with Your perfect love. Let it quiet every fear in me.

Journal Prompt

What fear can you release in exchange for God's perfect love today?

My Notes & Prayers

_____

_____

_____

_____

_____

Day 152: Sufficient Grace

Scripture

2 Corinthians 12:9

Reflection

God's grace is sufficient. Not just in theory—in your weakness, right now, today. His power shows up most when you feel least capable. So stop trying to be strong enough. Let grace hold you up. It's not about what you lack; it's about who He is.

Prayer

Jesus, Your grace is enough for me. Help me rest in that truth today.

Journal Prompt

Where do you feel weak—and how can grace meet you there?

My Notes & Prayers

_____

_____

_____

_____

_____

Day 153: Run Your Race

Scripture

Hebrews 12:1

Reflection

Let us run with endurance the race set before us. Not someone else's race—yours. Comparison is a thief of joy, but clarity comes when your eyes are on Jesus. Stay in your lane. Your journey is sacred, even if it looks different. Just keep running faithfully.

Prayer

Lord, help me focus on my race. Keep my eyes on You and not on others.

Journal Prompt

Where have you been comparing—and how can you return your gaze to Jesus?

My Notes & Prayers

_____

_____

_____

_____

_____

Day 154: Jesus Never Changes

Scripture

Hebrews 13:8

Reflection

Jesus Christ is the same yesterday, today, and forever. In a world that constantly shifts, He remains steady. When everything feels uncertain, He is your constant. Let His faithfulness ground you. You don't have to fear the future—because He's already there.

Prayer

Jesus, You never change. Help me anchor my life in Your unshakable truth.

Journal Prompt

What change in your life can you face with confidence in His consistency?

My Notes & Prayers

_____

_____

_____

_____

_____

Day 155: He Goes Before You

Scripture

Deuteronomy 31:8

Reflection

God goes before you. He's not just with you—He's ahead of you, preparing the way. There's no surprise waiting that will catch Him off guard. As you step into uncertainty, trust the One who's already there. He walks before you with wisdom, strength, and love.

Prayer

God, thank You for going before me. Help me walk in peace, knowing You've prepared the way.

Journal Prompt

Where do you need to trust that God is already working ahead of you?

My Notes & Prayers

_____

_____

_____

_____

_____

Day 156: Hope Does Not Disappoint

Scripture

Romans 5:5

Reflection

Hope in God is not wishful thinking—it's confidence rooted in His character. This kind of hope never puts you to shame. When you feel tempted to give up, remember: hope anchored in Jesus is never wasted. Let hope rise again today.

Prayer

Lord, restore my hope. Let me believe again in Your promises, even when I don't see results yet.

Journal Prompt

What is one thing you're still hoping for—and how can you renew that hope today?

My Notes & Prayers

_____

_____

_____

_____

_____

Day 157: God Finishes What He Starts

Scripture

Philippians 1:6

Reflection

God is faithful to complete the work He started in you. You are a work in progress, but He doesn't leave things undone. Even when it feels slow, He is moving. You are becoming the person He envisioned. Stay the course. He's not finished with you yet.

Prayer

Father, thank You that You finish what You start. Help me stay steady in the process of becoming.

Journal Prompt

What part of your journey needs the reminder that God is still working?

My Notes & Prayers

_____

_____

_____

_____

_____

Day 158: Joy Comes in the Morning

Scripture

Psalm 30:5

Reflection

Weeping may endure for a night, but joy comes in the morning. Grief is real, but it doesn't get the last word. God promises that joy is on the other side. If you're in a season of sorrow, hold on. The sun is rising. Joy is coming.

Prayer

Jesus, in my sorrow, remind me of the joy to come. Strengthen me to endure the night and welcome the morning.

Journal Prompt

What sorrow do you need to hand to God as you wait for joy to return?

My Notes & Prayers

_____

_____

_____

_____

_____

Day 159: A Future and a Hope

Scripture

Jeremiah 29:11

Reflection

God's plans for you are good—to give you a future and a hope. Even if your present feels messy, your story is not over. You are moving toward something redemptive. Cling to that promise today: God's heart toward you is always for hope.

Prayer

God, thank You for good plans. Give me eyes to see the hope You've planted in my future.

Journal Prompt

What part of your life needs to be reframed in light of God's hopeful plans?

My Notes & Prayers

_____

_____

_____

_____

_____

Day 160: It Is Finished

Scripture

John 19:30

Reflection

Jesus' final words on the cross remind us: it is finished. The striving, the earning, the weight of sin—it's all been handled. You can rest in the finished work of Christ. Live from victory, not for it. Your story ends in redemption.

Prayer

Jesus, thank You for finishing what I could never accomplish. Help me live in the freedom of Your finished work.

Journal Prompt

What burden can you release today, knowing Christ already carried it for you?

My Notes & Prayers

_____

_____

_____

_____

_____

A NEW SEASON

The Journey Continues...

160 days.

That's over five months of showing up, turning the page, and leaning into God's presence—day by day. You've walked through valleys and mountaintops, silence and songs, questions and confidence. You've sat with sorrow and risen in joy. You've heard the whisper of truth in dark nights and felt the strength of grace in weary moments.

This devotional was never about perfection—it was about presence. About learning to meet God not just in church pews or peaceful mornings, but in the chaos of family life, the ache of uncertainty, the grind of everyday routine. Through Scripture, reflection, and honest prayer, you've carved out space to encounter Him—and He showed up.

You've learned that:

You are seen—even in the wilderness.

You are loved—not for what you do, but for who you are.

You are held—when life falls apart.

You are being shaped—through trials and tenderness alike.

And above all, you are not alone.

Some days you may have felt nothing. Others may have brought tears or deep conviction. But every single day was another step forward—a seed planted, a truth remembered, a promise clung to.

This devotional may end here, but your journey with God does not. The pages may close, but His invitation remains open:

"Come to Me."

Every day. Every emotion. Every struggle. Come with your questions and your praise, your fears and your dreams. He is the same yesterday, today, and forever—and He walks with you still.

So go forward, not with pressure, but with peace. Not with striving, but with surrender. Keep showing up. Keep seeking. And let your life become the next page of this sacred journey.

You've come this far. And He's not finished yet.

My Notes & Prayers

✎ My Notes & Prayers

✍ My Notes & Prayers

My Notes & Prayers

🖊 My Notes & Prayers

My Notes & Prayers

My Notes & Prayers

My Notes & Prayers

My Notes & Prayers

My Notes & Prayers

✐ My Notes & Prayers

My Notes & Prayers

My Notes & Prayers

✍ My Notes & Prayers

My Notes & Prayers

✍ My Notes & Prayers

My Notes & Prayers

My Notes & Prayers

My Notes & Prayers

🖋 My Notes & Prayers

My Notes & Prayers

✍ My Notes & Prayers

My Notes & Prayers

My Notes & Prayers

www.ingramcontent.com/pod-product-compliance
Lightning Source LLC
Chambersburg PA
CBHW060150130626

46556CB00006B/2582